Encyclopedia Of Spiritual Development

Book Three

Pam Brittan

Encyclopedia of Spirit original copyright Pam Brittan 2013

Website: www.spiritenergyuk.co.uk

Email: pambrittan@spiritenergyuk.co.uk

Pam Brittan

All rights reserved.

DEDICATION

I dedicate this to all my family and friends and those who have supported be through my many years of working with Spirit.
Most of all I am humbled by the messages I have received from those in the Spirit World to enable me to collate this book for sale.

Foreword

As I produce each booklet I am amazed how much information I have gathered. So many wonderful and renowned Mediums in the past have gone without imparting their profound knowledge.

The courses I have developed overtime has made me realized the demand for wisdom and understanding is becoming more important in this material world where we all live, hence, why I felt the need to produce these various books to enable people to gain comprehension of their own gift.

This booklet contains some very profound learning—how the auric field is divided into layers and how this affects our moods and energy levels. I have touched upon the knowledge of Akashic Records which is sometimes too big a subject to comprehend, but believing it all takes a leap of faith. Remember these words "seeing is not believing—believing is seeing" Explaining about Mental Mediumship and Healing is on a more practical level.

The journey of life and experience takes us all to many levels, as we develop, and gain more awareness of possibilities and probabilities, our pathway begins to change. The lesson in life is whether we adapt and use the skills we have acquired or do we stay in the well trodden path we have created!!!!!

A rut we walk gets deeper the longer we walk along the track until eventually we may need a ladder to get out of the trench we have created. It does sometimes take faith and understanding that we are protected. Also having confidence that there is a Divine Source out there heeding our words and prayers.

No person should lecture another about what to believe, it has to come from a deep knowing within, something born within each of us. Sometimes this conviction comes later after many lessons, but, however it comes it is the beginning of a wonderful enlightenment.

It is not about religion, I respect all those that have a certain faith, but, it is more about spirituality and not judging others, a deep and hard lesson for us all.

Pam Brittan

Author

CONTENTS

Chapter One: Layers of the Auric Field

Chapter Two: The Akashic Records

Chapter Three: Mental Mediumship – Healing

As this is the third booklet of the series, reading this you have already gained a deal of knowledge. The subjects covered are very deep but I have tried to explain them in a down to earth way.

Each chapter contains a small section of how to practice with someone of like mind. This is very important at this stage of development. Especially trying to fathom the auric layers and getting to know more during the Healing section.

I have tried to give as much information about the subject of the Akashic Records as I can. It is only by gaining a little more knowledge about every subject that we will begin to understand more fully what these records are all about; because they are ongoing and expandable and retractable the same as our life journey.

As with every encyclopedia produced I want you to enjoy the learning process. Do not be too hard on yourself. I often say to my students just have an open mind and it will all happen. If you question everything and analyse all the time then you lose the ability to "tune" in. Give what you are getting but remember, to phrase it responsibly.

Basically there is no right or wrong way, there is only **THE WAY.** However, your gift is used, remember it is for the highest good for all. We are individuals and not clones of each other. Your guides and helpers choose to be your mentors and they choose you as you are.

SEE THE POSSIBILITIES IN YOURSELF!!!

Chapter One

Layers of the Auric Field

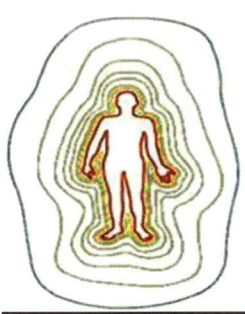

As we discussed before, who we are, everything we do, who we have been is in the Auric Field.

Some healers will penetrate the Aura of a person and perceive through an altered state of consciousness the different texture and essence of each layer.

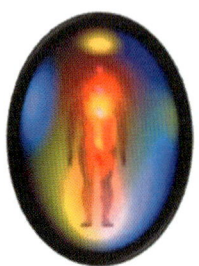

Each of the seven layers are associated with the seven chakras, and can glow with the colour of that chakra at times.

Hence the first layer is associated with the physical functioning and physical sensation – feeling physical pain or pleasure

The second layer and second chakra are in general associated with emotional aspect of human beings.

The third layer (solar plexus) is associated with mental life, with linear thinking.

The fourth is associated with the heart chakra the vehicle through which we love.

The fifth level is the level associated with a higher will – more connected with the divine.   The power of communication, speaking and listening is part of this level.

The sixth level and brow chakra are associated with celestial love connecting with overwhelming force of the universal energy

The seventh layer and crown chakra is associated with the higher mind. Understanding the concept of the layers within the Aura will help in the understanding of the nature of the human force both physically and psychically

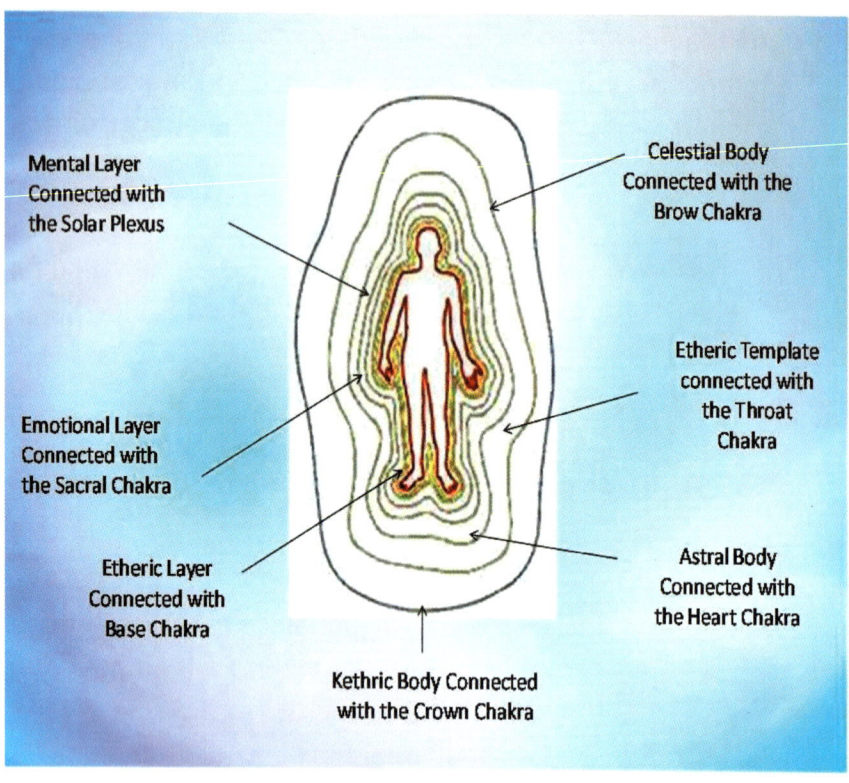

The Etheric Body (the first Layer)

The etheric body (from "ether" the state between energy and matter) is composed of tiny energy lines "like a sparkling web of light beams." Similar to the lines on a television screen.

The web-like structure of the etheric body is in constant motion. To clairvoyant vision, sparks of bluish-white light move along its energy lines throughout the entire dense physical body.

The etheric body extends from one quarter to two inches beyond the physical body and pulsates about 15 – 20 cycles per minute The colour varies from light blue to grey this first layer will duplicate the bodies energy and structure. If you were to see this without the body you would "see" it as a woman or a man.

The Emotional Body (The Second Layer)

The second Auric body is generally called the emotional body and is associated with feelings. It roughly follows the outline of the physical body. Its structure is much more fluid than the etheric and does not duplicate the physical body.

Rather it appears to be coloured clouds of fine substance in continual fluid motion. It extends one to three inches from the body. This layer contains all the colours of the rainbow and will vary upon the moods of the person.

The Mental Body (The Third Layer)

The third aura body is the mental body. The layer extends beyond the emotional and is composed of still finer substances, all of which are associated with thoughts and mental processes. This body usually appears as a bright yellow light radiating about the head and shoulders and extending around the whole body. It expands and becomes brighter when its owner is concentrating on mental processing.

It extends from three to eight inches from the body. In this energy you will perceive blobs of varying brightness and colour which are thought forms actually in the Auric field. It is to this body we will tune into to pick up on a psychic level what is going on with that person.

The Astral Body (The Fourth Layer)

The astral body is composed of clouds of colour more beautiful than those of the emotional body. The astral body tends to have the same set of colours, but they are usually infused with the rose light of love. It extends out about half to one foot from the body.

When someone falls in love there is an actual cord from the aura that mingles with the cord of the person they love – the longer the bond the stronger they get. Hence, when relationships end for whatever reason the pain caused can tear into your Auric field and take time to heal.

A great deal of interaction actually goes on between people on the astral level. Interaction between auras can certainly connect will produce blobs of colour being sent to the aura of the person who attracts you – even if that person is unaware of the attention at the time – they will feel someone looking or connecting with them.

The Etheric Template Body (Fifth Layer)

The etheric layer of the energy field drives its structure from the etheric template layer. It is the blueprint or the perfect form for the etheric layer to take.

This is the level where you are putting information of this lifetime!!!!

It extends between one to two feet. This layer appears as clear or transparent lines on the cobalt blue background, much like an architect's blueprint, only this blueprint exists in another dimension (your soul's Akashic Record – read this in the next chapter)

This is the information you came with so this is where you are adding the information of the present time!!!

The Celestial Body (Sixth Layer)

The sixth level is the emotional level of the spiritual plane, called the celestial body. It extends about two to three feet from the body. It is the level though which we experience spiritual rapture which can only be achieved with time, mediation and a realization of "being".

This level appears like a beautiful shimmering light with a gold/silver sheen. This is the layer of unconditional love with the knowledge of the universal energy and connection with "God"

The Kethric Template Or Causal Body (Seventh level)

The seventh level is the mental level of the spiritual plane called the kethric template. It extends from one to three feet from the body. When we bring our consciousness to the seventh level of the aura, we know that we are one with the Creator.

The outer form is the egg shape of the aura body and contains all the Auric bodies associated with the present incarnation and individual is undergoing. The egg appears golden and shimmering when you" see " it and appears like an egg shell protecting the Auric field.

The golden template levels also contain the main power current that runs up and down the spine and is the main power current that nourishes the whole body.

In addition, in the kethric template level are also the past life bands within the eggshell.

These are coloured bands of light which completely encircle the aura and can be found anywhere on the eggshell surface.

The band found near the head/neck is usually the band containing the past life that you are working to clear in your present life circumstance.

This level is the last Auric level in the spiritual plane, It contains the life plan and is the last level directly related to this incarnation. Beyond this level is the cosmic plane, the plane that cannot be experienced from the limiting view point of only one incarnation.

There are many people who actually see the auric field around a person or living entity, we all have this skill it is just understanding what we are seeing. This energy is also emitted by plants and animals. It has been proved scientifically that this energy exists with all living things.

Although we often ignore what is happening by thinking it is a trick of the light when we see colour around someone. I am not a person that often sees the aura rather I sense the energy but this is just as good and this is how we pick up information clairvoyantly.

A good practice now would be try to feel the different layers of the auric field with a like minded person. Place your hands gently into their energy field and feel the vibration of each level.

Your hands should get hot or cold, there may be tingling, you may feel different sensations the longer you penetrate the aura. Write down your experience and compare notes with each other. You may have very similar experiences and ideas where the change comes for each layer.

The aura is likened to Radio Wave patterns around the body emitting information for the person with the Auric field or the clairvoyant to receive and hear in order to give out the knowledge perceived.

The best way of trying to see this energy is asking someone to stand in front of a white or bland background then squint your eyes and see a haze around them. It does take practice and you can often see the auric field when you are in a darkened room and they stand with the light behind them (maybe through the open door).

The information of the different layers explains how the energies within us (the chakras) and around us can have an influence on our moods and how we react to people.

There are levels on the cosmic plane composed of very fine high vibrations, and are located above the head. They alternate between substance and form and hold more information about past life experiences.

Each level has a profound effect on our lives in this incarnation. We can access the information with the help of meditation and spiritual awareness.

Chapter Two

The Akashic Records

It is no exaggeration to state that the computer has transformed (and is still transforming) the planet. No segment of modern society has gone unaffected. The amount of information stored in computer memory and crossing the internet highway daily is literally unfathomable.

And yet, this vast complex of computer systems and collective databases cannot begin to come close to the power the memory, or the omniscient recording capacity of the Akashic Records.

For ease of understanding , the Akashic Records or "The Book of Life" can be likened to the universe's supercomputer system.

"Akasha" comes from the Sanskrit word meaning "boundless space" and is equated to the central storehouse of all information for every individual who has ever lived.

More than just a reservoir of events, The Akashic Records contain every deed, word, feeling, thought, and intent that has occurred at any time in the history of the world.

Much more than simply a memory storehouse, these Akashic Records are interactive: they have a tremendous influence upon our everyday lives, our relationships, our feelings and belief systems, and the potentials and probabilities we draw toward us.

The Akashic Records contain the history of every soul since the dawn of creation. These records connect each of us to one another. They contain the stimulus for every archetypal symbol or mythic story which has ever deeply touched patterns of human behaviour and experience.

They draw us toward or repel us from one another. They mould and shape levels of human consciousness. They are a portion of Divine Mind.

They are the unbiased judge and jury that attempt to guide, educate, and transform every individual to become the very best that she or he can be.

Imagine writing every deed, every thought, our history, our beliefs and every past and potential relationship we have down in a book, there would not be enough bookshelves to accommodate it all.

Information about these Akashic Records—this Book of Life—can be found in folklore, in myth, and throughout the Old and New Testaments. It is traceable at least as far back as the Semitic peoples and includes the Arabs, the Assyrians, the Phoenicians, the Babylonians, and the Hebrews.

Among each of these peoples was the belief that there is in existence some kind of celestial tablets which contain the history of humankind as well as all manner of spiritual information

For many individuals this Book of Life is simply a symbol of those destined for heaven and has its roots in the custom of recording genealogical records of names or perhaps early census taking.

Traditional religion suggests that this book—either in literal or symbolic form – contains the names of all those who are worthy of salvation, but, we have moved on from this theory today.

Closer to our current era, a great deal of contemporary information on the akashic Records has been made available by both reputable psychics and modern mystics.

According to Helena Petrovna Blavatsky (1831—1891),), a Russian immigrant, mystic, and founder of the Theosophical Society, the Akashic Records are much more than simply an account of static data which may be gleaned by a medium or sensitive. Instead, the records have an ongoing creative stimulus upon the present:

"Akasha is one of the cosmic principles and is a plastic matter, creative in its physical nature, immutable in its higher principles. It is the quintessence of all possible forms of energy, material, psychic, or spiritual; and contains within itself the germs of universal creation, which sprout forth under the impulse of the Divine Spirit"

In terms of contemporary insights, perhaps the most extensive source of information regarding the Akashic Records comes from the clairvoyant work of Edgar Cayce (1877—1945)

He would be able to access the Akashic Records during a trance like state.

When asked about the accuracy and source of the information Cayce replied that there were essentially two sources: the first was the subconscious mind of the individual for who he was giving the reading and the second was the Akashic Records

Individuals who wish to discover what is written about themselves on the Akashic Records may not have to look far for the answers. Cayce told one woman that the soul became aware of relevant information impressed on the Akashic Records whenever that individual applied whatever knowledge she or he possessed

Elsewhere, individuals were told that they couldn't help but encounter the information because "*these records were NOT as pictures on a screen, NOT as written words but are as ACTIVE FORCES in the life of an entity*".

When Edgar Cayce did his readings he was able to access the Akashic Records of past lives, present and future. Often we are living out something we did not resolve in a previous incarnation and accessing these records would enable Edgar Cayce to help conquer a fear or repeated behaviour pattern.

Regardless of what relationship, experience, or challenge we are currently in, it is that very same experience which the Akashic Records have brought into manifestation.

What we do with that situation remains a matter of free will, but the potential for soul growth is ever present.

The Edgar Cayce readings suggest that each of us writes the story our lives through our thoughts, our deeds, and our interactions with the rest of creation. This information has an effect upon us in the here and now

In fact, the Akashic Records have such an impact upon our lives and the potentials and probabilities we draw toward us that any exploration of them cannot help but provide us with insights into the nature of ourselves and our relationship to the universe.

There is much more to our lives, our histories, and our individual influence upon our tomorrows than we have perhaps dared to imagine

LIFE ISN'T ABOUT FINDING YOURSELF

LIFE IS ABOUT CREATING YOURSELF

By accessing information from the Akashic Records, the universe's computer database, much might be revealed to us.

The world as we have collectively perceived is but a faint shadow of reality.

A question for debate is whether our destiny is mapped out and do these records hold what is in store for this lifetime.

Do we really have free will?

Remember, past lives do have an influence on what happens this life journey!

The influence we have on others and they on us is limitless and it is when we realise this information has an impact on how the people of the world have an integral part on each other.

We must all remember the words uttered by Saint Teresa of Calcutta *"the world will only be at peace when we remember that we all belong to each other"*

All of us have the capability to meditate and delve into our own Akashic Record. It is with patience and allowing the meditation to go deep within and bringing forth the information we have bought with us when we have come onto this earth plane.

Remember the information about the Layers in the Auric Field part of those layers have the information we need.

A person frightened of confined spaces may have brought that fear from a previous lifetime and had never dealt with it then; the fear may have come about by a child being locked in a cellar or cupboard. This lifetime there is a need to handle this fear and bring about a resolution and calm to enable the person not to be intimidated by closed areas.

Find a time to meditate and practice going within and asking those guides and helpers to give you information you need from your akashic record. Something which relates to this lifetime you are living now!

Maybe you have already gleaned some because you are already living the pathway with a "knowing". Access more by simply asking for the information to come forward.

Chapter Nine

Mental Mediumship – Healing

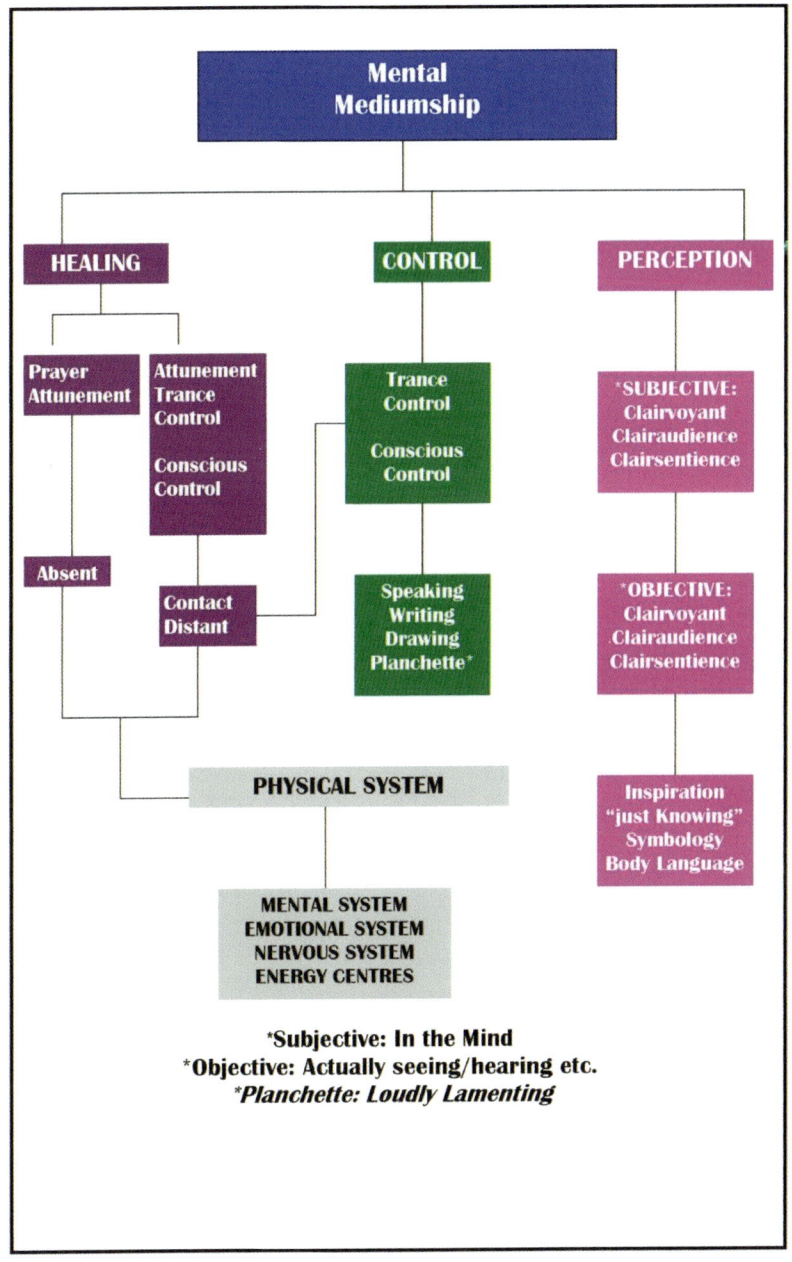

As you can see by the diagram, Mental Mediumship covers the aspects of Healing, Control, and Perception. In the following book I give information to help you understand the aspect of Trance and Clairvoyance, which is part of the Control and Perception.

In this chapter we are talking about the Healing side of Mental Mediumship. The diagram shows that prayer and absent healing is very much a part of the whole healing process. Prayer conjures up a religious perspective, but this is a word that means entreaty, plea, hope and appeal. When we are using prayer in this context we mean just that - we are sending our energy to help the healing of another by appealing to a higher force, a divine source for that to happen.

There are many types of healing some of which are spiritual, Reiki, crystal and colour. If healing is your pathway then you have a wonderful gift to enable the help to go to many people.

Many healers can do their work in a trance like state which enables them to "tune in" to the auric field and the chakra system to find the area which needs healing.

Often they are guided towards the spot and can give great comfort to the recipient. When healing takes place under conscious control this just means you are being guided to the zone needing healing by instinctive methods (as well as those divine sources who help).

This does have a effect on the Healers themselves by drawing on their physical system as shown in the Diagram. When training to do healing one of the most important factors is knowing how to protect your own energy.

In simple terms it is a form of mediumship that allows people in the Spirit world to direct their healing energies to people here in the physical world. These energies have the capability to affect the human form on all levels, physical, mental, emotional and spiritual. (see diagram)

The healing energies come from "The Source". The Divine Energy some called the God essence. This is nothing new; there has always been and always will be available to those who have the ability to allow this to happen.

The phenomena of 'healing hands' has been written about for many thousands of years, you only have to read about historical events either in the Bible or many history books to see this.

I believe that everyone has the gift to access these energies to some degree. However, as with all natural abilities some will have a greater power than others.

Regardless of age, religion, race or creed we all have the ability to help heal ourselves by balancing the subtle energies within and around our bodies. For thousands of years human beings have been aware of the health benefits gained by working with physical, mental, emotional and spiritual healing energy.

In recent years there has been renewed interest in accessing these ancient healing energies - and for good reason.

A crucial factor in this process is the relationship between the Medium (healer) and those in the Spirit world who access the energies at the source. If we accept that the Spirit doctors are experts, then all we need to do is learn how to simply allow them to do it.

There is a further belief that the relationship between the medium and the Spirit healer has a direct and proportional effect on what can be achieved for the patient.

The whole purpose of the exercise, is to be of service to the Divine Spirit, the Spirit world and the patients that need healing.

So, what is the healing mediums job? As strange as it may sound it is not to try to heal people. If you focus your attention on the patient, you will simply give your own energy, and we call that magnetic or psychic healing. This is a simple transference of vital energy from you to the patient. It will uplift and give them a boost, but it is non-specific and will only have a general uplifting effect. Further if you do this over an extended period of time you will deplete your own reserves and become quite tired and run down.

The medium's job is to learn how to raise their vibrational rate to get a link with the Spirit doctor. Therefore the focus of attention is not on the patient, but exactly the opposite, on the Spirit world.

If the mediums job is to simply link with the Spirit world, how do we do this and once we learn that, how can we develop it? The answer to that lies through personal development groups and training courses.

This talks very much about the Spiritual aspect of the healing process, but, as with this gift all healing follows a very similar process. Whichever course you follow will produce a different way to approach the healer/patient empathy. The distinct aspect of all healing is the Divine Source which helps that healing process.

As the medium's ability develops they are able to access more and more effective and profound energies. This in turn has a greater Healing effect upon the patient. The chart shows 7 levels of healing mediumship

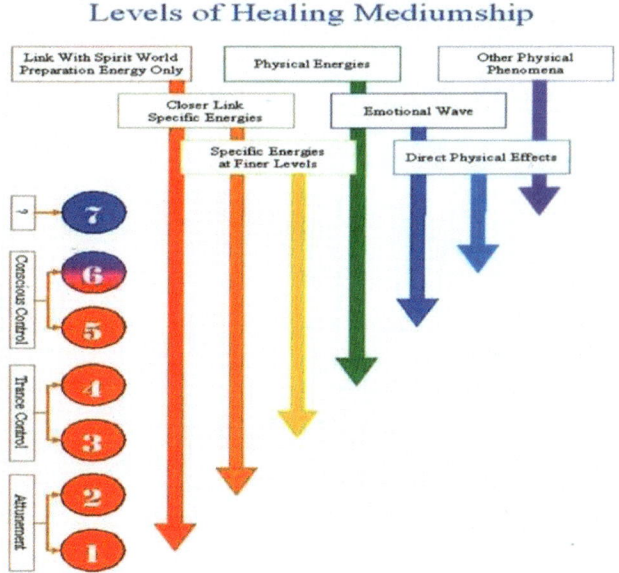

As you can see by the chart at stage 1 and 2 this is the beginning of the attuning process—the healer is trying to connect with their guides and helpers and also "tune" in to the patient, and where their problem is on the body.

Stages 3 and 4 starts the process of going into a trance like

state during the healing which in turn has an effect of the physical energies of both patient and healer. Often at this stage the Healer can be unaware of the power he/she is giving to the patient.

Stages 5 and 6 the healer is now back to a more conscious level of healing, and is becoming aware of the change in the patient's energy.

At Level 7 the healer is now aware of the deep emotional effect he/she has had on the recipient.

To try to experience the healing aspect of mediumship, get together with a like minded person. Get them to sit on a chair with their back at the side of the chair rather than the back, this will enable easier access to the person's back and sides.

In this practice, try to avoid around the head area. You do not want the patient to go so deep you cannot bring them around so until you gain experience and qualify as a healer it is best to do this practice with that very much in mind. Be in a quiet room, play music which will enable meditation.

Before you enter into this ask permission of your "patient" put your hands into the energy field around them at their side, back and front. There is no need to lay hands on at this stage, again, this is for the more experienced healer. During this process take note of how you feel as the healer, ask your patient to take note of how they feel and compare notes afterwards.

What was happening? Did the patient feel hot or cold? Did

you as the healer feel where they had a particular problem? Swop places and experience being the patient. Enjoy the energy you both receive and give. Afterwards wash your hands to clear the energy. This is a precious gift, and if this is your pathway find the group or teacher to help you qualify.

What is Distant Healing?

Distant healing is healing performed when the patient is not present. It is possible to transmit healing energies over any distance and this form of healing can be very effective.

The patients may or may not be aware that this healing has been undertaken for them but may attain much benefit from it coming as it does from the love and concern that their friends and relatives have for them.

Many Churches have Healing Books where people can put in the names of those that need healing. During the services or at a designated time the healing is sent absently and the energy will go to the person in need.

Absent or Distant healing is a great way of sending to your loved ones or animals the source energy of healing. I have been targeted with this healing and have felt the benefit.

Healing is not about curing it is about bringing peace and understanding. At no time must a Healer encourage a patient on prescription drugs not to take the medication or cease attending medical appointments. As with all mediumship you must take the responsibility of your gift.

This is so important. You cannot perform miracles, that is in the hands of the Divine. You can only be of service and what is meant to be, will be. When someone is nearing the end of their time on this earth sometimes the healing helps makes the transition easier.

Healing is a wonderful gift. Do not doubt the power you are given. Always be well prepared: prepare your room, yourself and your patient.

Be Humble your gift has been given to you, but, if you are not worthy it can be taken away again. So remember:

RESPONSIBILITY

HUMBLENESS

PREPARATION

In each book I will remind you to protect your energy, this is doubly important when you are healing. The chapters in this booklet contain some very useful and profound information.

Many years ago I had a reading with a man who said he could read souls, at the time I did not take much notice of this claim. I realise now with the knowledge I have; he was accessing my Akashic Record, he told me I had been prevented in previous lives to fulfill my purpose but, this time I would do this and my name would be known for the knowledge I imparted. This was many years before I began my journey of being a Medium.

At the time my children were young and I thought "what a load of nonsense, what could I possibly know".

Some of the things he said now make sense, but at the

time, I didn't even want that reading it was through a good friend of mine and I was curious. Again, it was no coincidence, I was meant to hear that information and even dismiss it at the time.

Pathways are created we just have to trust we are doing the right thing at the right time with the right person.

I have had a very chequered life from birth, I often say it reads like a Catherine Cookson novel. My experiences have meant that I have an empathy with people and maybe this was also meant to be.

Do not become bitter about things that have happened, ask yourself what lesson you have learnt by what occurred and how can you make it better not just for yourself but for others around you.

Our pathway is full of rocks and boulders, some of it because of past life karma. So let this life be a great learning experience and enjoy the ride.

Book Four:

Mental Mediumship: Perception and Control

Physical Mediumship: Apports, Ectoplasm, Materialization, Transfiguration, Percussion, Levitation, Direct Voice, Independent Voice, Slate Writing, Spirit Painting

My life now is about service for the greater good; but that has not come easy and I am still working on being the best I can in Spirit's Name.. Teaching is very important to me but I can only do that if the pupil is willing and able to have an open and enquiring mind.

There are no right or wrong answers if information given resonates with you then it is right. It is practice and knowledge that can help in these situations.

Open our eyes, and ears, our minds and remember our thoughts live and breathe and are us; so think positively about others, try not to judge and allow yourself to be accepting of everything that is right.!!!!!

Chinese proverb:

>   Do not falter in the dark—light a candle

>   Wise words!

>   Love and light

>   Pam Brittan

Printed in Great Britain
by Amazon.co.uk, Ltd.,
Marston Gate.